SUBSTANCE
USE DISORDERS

Participant Workbook

A Court-Approved Guide to Understanding, Managing, and Overcoming Substance Use Challenges

Dr. Arleen A. Fuller, Ph.D.

TABLE OF CONTENTS

PERCEPTION

How we view or see things can influence our thought process and behavior. Inaccurate perceptions of situations can lead to negative thinking, negative behavior, and negative consequences. There is power in perception. Have you ever viewed something as hard to achieve and then when you tried it, it was easy? Or have you ever viewed something as easy and it was actually hard? Or have you ever had the wrong perception of someone or something? We have to be mindful of our perceptions. Everything is not always what it seems to be and we need to make sure that we are looking through the right lens.

1. What is your perception of being in treatment? Please be honest.

_____

_____

_____

_____

_____

_____

2. How did you come to this conclusion? Is it based on your personal experience or what others have told you?

_____

_____

_____

_____

_____

_____

3. Do you have the right perception? Are you looking through the right lens?

_____

_____

_____

_____

4. Many people say that "seeing is believing." What does that statement mean to you?

_____

_____

_____

_____

_____

The statement "seeing is believing" is based on perception. Some people will never recover from addiction because they don't see themselves being clean in the future. They never visualized what a sober version of themselves looks like. They are okay with being an addict because they perceive it as being acceptable they will rationalize or defend their choices. They may even believe or perceive that recovery is difficult and does not have value, so they don't really try.

5. What perception do you have of yourself? What do you believe about yourself? Please be honest.

_____

_____

_____

_____

_____

_____

6. What does your ideal-self look or act like?

_____

_____

_____

_____

_____

_____

Self-Actualization

Create a plan and write down the things that you can do now to become your ideal-self.

_____

_____

_____

_____

_____

_____

There is power in perception

"Many capitalize on opportunities because of perception and many miss out on opportunities because of perception."

1. Some brand named clothes or shoes are viewed a certain way because of perception. How was this perception developed?

_____

_____

_____

_____

_____

2. What behaviors or perceptions have been promoted or marketed to you by your friends, family, and co-workers? What have you taken ownership of? Many perceptions are considered to be learned behavior. Are these perceptions right or wrong? Give us examples.

_____

_____

_____

_____

_____

_____

3. Explain this statement: "People want what they can't have." Are things perceived to be more appealing if it is deemed illegal, taboo, or limited?

_____

_____

_____

_____

_____

_____

"Many view abstaining from alcohol and drugs as hard, while others view it as easy. Both parties are right."

4. Is perception reality? Explain.

_____

_____

_____

_____

_____

_____

5. Sometimes having the wrong perception can trigger people to use drugs or alcohol. Has this ever happened to you? If so, what can you do to make sure this doesn't happen again?

_____

_____

_____

_____

_____

6. What is the difference between being rational and irrational?

_____

_____

_____

_____

_____

_____

7. Is irrational behavior a gift or a curse? Please explain.

_____

_____

_____

_____

_____

8. What can you do to make sure you make rational choices?

_____

_____

_____

_____

_____

9. Please explain how using illegal drugs or abusing alcohol is going to improve your health, income, family, and ability to remain free from incarceration.

_____

_____

_____

_____

_____

10. How do you perceive someone that is an addict?

_____

_____

_____

_____

_____

_____

11. Based on your description, would you consider yourself to be an addict? Please explain why or why not.

_____

_____

_____

_____

_____

_____

12. Many people say "I don't care what other people think." But for many, that is not true. What strategies can you use to keep a positive mindset if someone perceives you the wrong way?

_____

_____

_____

_____

_____

_____

13. If you were to continue to abuse alcohol or illegal drugs, what would be the possible consequences of your actions?

_____

_____

_____

_____

_____

_____

RELAPSE PREVENTION PLAN

Relapse Prevention Plans are created to assist in monitoring behavior patterns and gives you the ability to make adjustments. This tool will assist you in examining your behavior and creating positive alternative choices when you are triggered to do something negative due to your emotions. Please write down your triggers and your usual response to them. After that is complete, write down the same triggers and a positive alternative response for each trigger.

Trigger	Negative Response
Example: Failure	Response: Go get drunk

Trigger	Positive Response
Example: Failure	Response: I'm going to view this as a learning experience and I understand that even geniuses fail. Now is not the time to be irrational and find an excuse to drink. I will take a break and do something that improves my mood. When I am ready, I will try again.

	8

FOLLOW THE SIGNS

What is the purpose of street signs? Street signs give us direction. These signs tell us what the speed limit is and whether we should go or stop. Some signs tell us to slow down and alert us if there is a railroad crossing ahead. Signs warn us of danger and inform us that we should be cautious. If we choose to ignore these signs, we could potentially crash and face severe injury or possible death.

Our life is no different. We are given signs but sometimes we choose to ignore them. This is why our lives end up in a wreck. We fail to follow the signs. Sometimes signs lead us in a certain direction but we keep on detouring because we are hard headed and would rather take the long route. Why go through this? Why waste time and energy? When I was growing up my dad used to always tell me, "You can learn the easy way, or you can learn the hard way." At 35 years old, I now choose the easy way. Many of us can see signs from a distance. A smart man learns from his mistakes and a genius learns from other's mistakes.

AVOIDING TRIGGERS

You may have heard some people that are in recovery say "be smart, not strong." This implies that we can avoid relapsing or returning to negative behavior patterns by using better judgment. If we are smart, we do not have to be strong. Certain people, places, or things can trigger negative behavior patterns or relapse. By placing yourself in these situations, it will require you to be strong. Many of us think we are strong, but we are really not. Choose to be smart and avoid your triggers.

In the boxes below, please list the people, places, and things that you need to avoid.

People	Places	Things

STAYING BUSY

Cravings can start from a bad feeling that you want to escape or a good feeling that you want to experience. Substance use serves as immediate gratification to satisfy emotional needs.

Stage 1 – Depression, Anxiety, Stress, Anger, Grief, Celebration, Etc.

Stage 2 – Desire to release the bad feeling or feel the good feeling by using

Stage 3 – Fantasizing about the emotional lift it may give

Stage 4 – The urge to use grows

Stage 5 – Rationalize using

Stage 6 – Planning to use

Stage 7 – Using drugs or alcohol

***Many people also use because they are bored. This is not acceptable and it is not an excuse to use. Find alternate activities that stimulate your mind and make you feel good.

Place a checkmark next to the things that interest you.

_____ Fishing	_____ Travel	_____ Volunteering
_____ Hiking	_____ Investing	_____ Exercise
_____ Video Games	_____ Art	_____ Writing
_____ Puzzles	_____ Inventing	_____ Flying
_____ Magic	_____ Design	_____ Diving
_____ Collectables	_____ Scrapbooking	_____ Racing
_____ Athletics	_____ Business	_____ Programming
_____ Tutoring	_____ Organizing	_____ Other

DENIAL

Denial is something that we must address in treatment. There are those in group that will give a million excuses to why they do the things that they do. They will rationalize their behavior and defend choices by bringing up statistics, laws in other countries, scientific studies, etc. Most of them know what they are saying is full of you-know-what. They are not fooling the counselor or the people around them. They are just fooling themselves.

What are you in denial about? This does not have to be necessarily related with substance use. Here are a list of things that some people are in denial about:

Relationships

Eating Habits

Getting Older

Exercising

Family History

School Work

Substance Use

Career Choice

Fame

Spending Habits

Illness

Work Ethic

Their Children

Appearance

1. Can you add to this list? What are people in denial about?

_____

_____

_____

_____

_____

2. Why do you think some people live in denial?

_____

_____

_____

_____

_____

_____

3. Is this healthy?

   Yes or No

4. What are you in denial about? Are you going to stay in denial or change?

_____

_____

_____

_____

_____

_____

5. Does denial truly help you? Please explain

_____

_____

_____

_____

_____

_____

6. What would you like to change? Put a check next to all that apply to you.

_____

_____

_____

_____

_____

_____

_____ Substance Use	_____ Negative Thinking
_____ Financial Management	_____ Excessive Spending
_____ Peer Group	_____ Spouse
_____ Abusive Behavior	_____ Physical Health
_____ Jealousy and Envy	_____ Career
_____ Resentment	_____ Work Environment
_____ Commitment	_____ Self-Talk
_____ Decision Making	_____ Values
_____ Temperament	_____ Education Level
_____ Discipline	_____ Thought Process
_____ Mental Health	_____ Criminal Behavior

CHANGE YOUR ENVIRONMENT

You have possibly heard the saying, "They're a product of their environment." For many, this is true. But there are exceptions to this rule. Your mindset will always determine your future. But being in a healthy, positive environment can make life easier. But also remember that if you have not changed your mindset, you will attract the same negative people, places and things, no matter where you are.

For the sake of this workbook, I am going to suggest that you consider changing your environment. This can do wonders. Someone once told me, "If you stay in the barbershop long enough, eventually you will get a haircut."

"Birds of a feather flock together." Who are you flocking with? Whoever they are, make sure that they have their stuff together. If you cannot find anyone to hang out with, it's okay to ride solo. Sometimes our friends or associates can be major distractions.

Spend time with those who are smarter, wiser and more successful than you. Pick their brains for information and develop their habits if you are serious about changing.

STAGES OF CHANGE

Stage 1: Pre-contemplation (Not Ready)

Individuals do not see their behavior as a problem in this stage. Those in the Pre-contemplation stage do not intend to take action in the foreseeable future, even if they have experienced negative consequences for their actions.

Stage 2: Contemplation (Getting Ready)

Contemplation is the stage in which people are aware of the pros and cons of changing their behavior. Instead of defending their behavior, they evaluate, and consider the idea of changing. Continuously weighing the costs and benefits of changing can produce chronic contemplation or procrastination.

Stage 3: Preparation

Preparation is the stage to take action and do specific things that promote change. These individuals have a plan of action, such as going to therapy, talking to their physician, buying a self-help book, scheduling, creating a budget, etc.

Stage 4: Action

Action is the stage in which people have made specific, overt modifications in their lifestyles. Observers from the outside, like friends, relatives, and co-workers will notice that change is occurring. Specific actions are taken to promote lifestyle changes.

Stage 5: Maintenance

Maintenance is the stage in which people have made positive lifestyle choices and have been successful at avoiding relapse. While in the Maintenance stage, people are less tempted to relapse and grow increasingly more confident that they can continue their changes.

What stage of change are you in for the selection that applied to you?

_____ Substance Use		_____ Discipline
_____ Financial Management		_____ Mental Health
_____ Peer Group		_____ Negative Thinking
_____ Abusive Behavior		_____ Excessive Spending
_____ Jealousy and Envy		_____ Spouse
_____ Resentment		_____ Physical Health
_____ Commitment		_____ Career
_____ Decision Making		_____ Work Environment
_____ Temperament		_____ Self-Talk

_____ Values   _____ Thought Process

_____ Education Level   _____ Criminal Behavior

How can you improve your weak areas?

_____

_____

_____

_____

_____

_____

MOTIVATION TO CHANGE

Motivation to change usually occurs when there is a perceived purpose or benefit to change. Many people minimize their behavior, make multiple excuses, or say "Why should I change?" In the back of their minds, they know that change requires work and they have become comfortable with their habits.

Change requires discipline and work. Everyone likes a job with benefits. But to get the benefits, you have to do the work. In this section, we want you to weigh the long-term pros and cons of changing your behavior. We want you to find your purpose.

Pros	Cons

Pros	Cons

ACCOUNTABILITY PARTNERS

Sometimes we need assistance in being accountable for our action or inaction. Accountability partners can help us stay on track with our goals by checking our progress. They tell us what we need to hear, not what we want to hear. Accountability partners tell us the truth and do not give us an excuse to relapse. Accountability partners are not enablers or those that we develop a co-dependency with. They are invested in our long-term success and sobriety. They can be friends, family members, co-workers, or sponsors from Alcoholics Anonymous or Narcotics Anonymous.

Write down the qualities of a great accountability partner.

_____

_____

_____

_____

_____

_____

Do you feel it is important for someone to hold you accountable?

Yes or No

Write down names of potential accountability partners who you trust to hold you accountable. Be careful in who you choose. Everyone is not meant to be an accountability partner. The person you choose may have great qualities, but may not be great in holding people accountable.

Potential Accountability Partners	What qualities do they have?

SELF-ESTEEM

Self-esteem is a term in psychology to reflect a person's overall evaluation or appraisal of his or her own worth. Low self-esteem affects both males and females. Although self-esteem is rarely discussed as a male issue, men and boys are also affected by low self-esteem.

1. How does someone with low self-esteem behave?

_____

_____

_____

_____

_____

_____

2. How does someone with healthy self-esteem behave?

_____

_____

_____

_____

_____

_____

3. What is the difference between healthy self-esteem and arrogance?

_____

_____

_____

_____

_____

_____

4. Sometimes those with low self-esteem try to bully, abuse, or talk down to others. Why do you think they do this? Have you ever experienced this? If so, how did this affect you or others?

_____

_____

_____

_____

_____

_____

5. How do you deal with bullies at the workplace?

_____

_____

_____

_____

_____

_____

6. What advice can you give to help others improve their self-esteem?

_____

_____

_____

_____

_____

_____

Strategies to Improve Self-Esteem

✓   Pursue easy goals
    Start with something you can accomplish easily. When we achieve small successes, it builds our confidence and momentum to go after bigger goals.

✓ Socialize

Get out of the house and practice your communication and interpersonal skills. Don't be afraid to engage in conversations. Others may be just as nervous as we are and do not express it. We are not alone. Some people are magicians and we only see what they allow us to see. Hang around people that have your best interests in mind and give constructive, honest, reliable feedback.

✓ Face your fears

It is important for us to face our fears so we can grow. By repeatedly facing our fears our irrational beliefs diminish and we gain confidence and courage. Haters see something in you that they cannot do themselves. Sometimes they want you to be fearful, just like them. It makes them comfortable to know that they are not alone. Some will try to tear you down or talk you out of pursuing your dreams so they can stop feeling inadequate when they are next to you. But you are better than this. It can be challenging to be optimistic if you feel that you are alone. But you are not alone. Many have conquered the same struggles, insecurities, fears and doubts that you now face.

✓ Build on your strengths

Do things on a regular basis that comes natural for you. Doing things that you are good at reinforces belief in your abilities and strengths. You can also add to your skills by taking advanced coursework or certification training in your field of study.

✓ Stop comparing yourself to others

Stop comparing yourself to other people. Low self-esteem stems from the feeling of being inferior. For example, if you were the only person in the world, do you think you could have low self-esteem? Self-esteem only comes into the picture when there are other people around us and we perceive that we are inferior. Don't worry about what your neighbor is doing. Accept that it'll serve you more to just go down your own path at your own pace rather than to compare yourself.

✓ Know thyself

Know who you are and do things that you are good at. Always try to put yourself in a position to win. Do things that you naturally excel in to build your confidence.

✓ Create a vision of yourself

Use your imagination and create an image of yourself as the confident and self-assured person you aspire to become. When you are this person, how will you feel? How will others perceive you? What does your body language look like? How will you talk? Feel the emotions, experiences, and daydream about your ideal life.

✓ Help others achieve their goals

Helping others achieve their goals can be fulfilling. It puts a smile on their face and can make you feel good as well. Plus if you help them with their goals, maybe they will help you with your goals.

✓ Create a plan

Having a goal is not enough. You need to have an action plan. Get moving and follow the steps that you need to take to achieve your goals.

✓ Get motivated

Be purpose driven. Have a reason why you are doing something. Associate yourself with people or things that inspire you. If you desire to be motivated, use this formula: High Emotion + Strong Purpose = Motivation

✓ Improve self-talk

Sometimes we have internal thoughts that are negative and irrational. We have to manage our self-talk and reinforce positive thoughts that improve our perspective. Internally, we can say good things about ourselves and build a positive image. Try to be optimistic and confident at all times. Monitor your self-talk and do not doubt yourself. Sometimes we need to keep things to ourselves. It is our duty to protect our minds from being polluted by negativity, doubt and fear from other people. Don't be affected by subliminal hate (facial expressions, sabotage, passive aggressive behavior, etc.) and maintain your drive.

Affirm your belief in yourself. Turn your passwords into affirmations for your email, social media, and personal accounts. This is one way you can try to reprogram your self-talk. For example, your password for your email account could be "I am confident and successful." Now every time you log in to one of your accounts you will always have to affirm to yourself that you are confident and successful.

✓ Be positive

There are many people that allow negative energy to transfer into their lives. Know that it is okay to smile and people are attracted to happy people. Do not allow negative people to transfer their energy into you. Just because they are mad does not mean that you have to be. There are no benefits in being negative.

PERSONAL ADVICE

Imagine that you are five years in the future and you have to write a letter to your present self. What advice would you give?

_____

_____

_____

_____

_____

_____

_____

_____

_____

_____

_____

_____

_____

_____

_____

_____

_____

_____

_____

_____

_____

_____

FORGIVENESS

Forgiveness is one of the hardest things to do. Letting go of the past and removing resentment is healthy. There are no benefits to holding on to grudges and past hurts. It's like driving a car while looking through the rearview mirror. Eventually, you will crash.

1. Who do you need to forgive and why?

Family   Friends   Co-workers   Spouse   Children   Yourself

_____

_____

_____

_____

_____

_____

_____

2. Do you forgive and forget? Or do you forgive and not forget?

_____

_____

_____

_____

_____

_____

_____

3. Is making amends important to you? If so, who do you need to say sorry to, and why?

_____

_____

_____

_____

_____

_____

_____

_____

4. What does true forgiveness look, act, and sound like?

_____

_____

_____

_____

_____

_____

_____

_____

5. After you forgive someone, does that mean you should still associate yourself with them?

_____

_____

_____

_____

_____

_____

_____

_____

_____

_____

_____

LIVING BY PRINCIPLES

It is important to have principles. Principles are the governors of your values and protect the things that you care about the most. The principles that you create will help you when you need to make tough decisions.

Values

Freedom

Principle: I do not hang out with people who sell or use drugs.

This protects my freedom, life, and family.

Career

Principle: I attend trainings quarterly to improve my skill level.

This helps my career and shows that I am committed.

Reputation

Principle: I always provide quality service.

This protects my reputation and increases my earning potential.

List the things that you value.

1._____

2._____

3._____

4._____

Now write down principles that protect those values.

1._____

..._____

..._____

2._____

..._____

..._____

3._____

..._____

..._____

4._____

..._____

..._____

What is your overall view of yourself physically, emotionally, and intellectually?

Physically I am:

_____   _____

_____   _____

_____   _____

_____   _____

Emotionally I am:

_____   _____

_____   _____

_____   _____

_____   _____

Intellectually I am:

_____   _____

_____   _____

_____   _____

_____   _____

Spiritually I am:

_____   _____

_____   _____

_____   _____

_____   _____

Write down a list of "shoulds" that you have based on your family, friends, culture, spirituality, media, music, school system, and any other areas. Which of these beliefs are rational and which are irrational? Place an "R" next the beliefs that you think are rational and an "I" next to the beliefs that you deem irrational. Place an "X" next to the statements that describe who you are currently.

		R or I	I am
Example:	I should be skinny	__R__	__X__
	I should be perfect	__I__	____
	I should be married by now	__I__	____

	R or I	I am
I should get all A's	__R__	____
I should _____	____	____
I should _____	____	____
I should _____	____	____
I should _____	____	____
I should _____	____	____
I should _____	____	____
I should _____	____	____
I should _____	____	____
I should _____	____	____
I should _____	____	____

Write down as many great things about yourself that you can think of in the next 2 minutes.

_____   _____

_____   _____

_____   _____

_____   _____

_____   _____

_____   _____

Write down as many not-so-great things about yourself that you can think of in the next 2 minutes.

_____   _____

_____   _____

_____ _____
_____ _____
_____ _____
_____ _____
_____ _____

Now analyze your two lists. Was it more difficult to write one list than the other? Which list is longer? Why do you think that is?

_____

_____

_____

_____

_____

Write a list of things that people have told you about yourself. Place an "X" next to the statements that you either agree or disagree with.

Example:	Agree	Disagree
I am an excellent writer.	__X__	_____
I am lazy.	__X__	_____
_____	_____	_____
_____	_____	_____
_____	_____	_____
_____	_____	_____
_____	_____	_____
_____	_____	_____

When I look in the mirror, I see_____

_____

How can you improve your self-image?

_____

_____

_____

_____

_____

_____

If you really dedicate yourself, what can you accomplish?

_____

_____

_____

_____

_____

_____

_____

_____

_____

_____

_____

_____

_____

_____

_____

_____

_____

_____

MOOD MANAGEMENT STRATEGIES

Music – Listen to enjoyable music. Listening to your favorite songs can improve your mood. Music is a powerful tool that has been used in movies to enhance emotions of fear, joy, sadness, excitement, etc. Imagine watching a scary movie without background music or sound effects. It wouldn't be as scary. You can use music to change your mood.

Nostalgia – Reminisce about happy times in your past. Review old pictures, movies, or television series that you used to enjoy. Do things that you used to enjoy, that you don't do now.

Self-Care – Take care of yourself. Get a massage, pedicure, manicure, etc. Go on vacation and eat healthy food. Exercise to increase your production of endorphins. With high endorphin levels, we feel less pain and fewer negative effects of stress. Endorphins have been suggested as modulators of the so-called "runner's high" that athletes achieve with prolonged exercise.

Self-Talk – Monitor or be mindful of what you say to yourself. Try to be positive and say things to yourself that uplift you instead of bring you down. Negative self-talk is not healthy and can destroy your life.

Journaling – Write down what is on your mind. By journaling, you can evaluate your life and express yourself honestly. Act out your emotions on paper. Later, you can review your entries and decide if you were being rational or being irrational. You can review your journal to remind yourself of previous accomplishments, lessons, and how you have overcome obstacles. Journaling is a great tool for personal growth.

Change Environment – Some people live, work, or go to school in negative environments. You would be surprised how exposure to different people, places, or things can improve your life. If you are in a negative environment, consider changing it to a positive one. Your odds of living a happy life increase when you are in a positive environment.

Counseling – Sometimes people become overwhelmed and are unable to cope with life's stressors. If this is the case for you, consider seeing a counselor. A professional counselor can assist you with challenging issues in your life. Receiving guidance from a neutral party who has no emotional attachment to the situation may bring clarity.

Stress Prevention Strategies – Do things ahead of time in order to prevent future stressful events from occurring. We want you to anticipate needs. Examples include: budgeting, planning ahead, paying bills on time, leaving early from work to avoid traffic, getting things done before you are asked, telling people "no," etc.

Things that can influence your mood

Caffeine	Thirst
Food	Clothes
Pictures	Heat
Scents	Noise
Hunger	Music

Silence	Stress/Pressure
Looking Good	Animals
Looking Bad	Children
Brightness	Accomplishment
Dimness	Someone else's vibes
Humor	Nostalgia
People	Massage
Rest	Color
Events	Puzzles
Colors	Adversity
Exercise	Opportunity
Finances	Injustice
(Dis) Satisfaction with life	Prejudice
Grooming	Alcohol
Cleanliness	Drugs
Body Image	Gambling
Sex	Shopping/Shoplifting
Health	Winning
Love	Losing

EMOTIONAL INTELLIGENCE

Emotional intelligence (EI) is the ability to perceive, control and evaluate emotions in yourself and others. EI is also ability to understand verbal and nonverbal communication that is presented in any given situation. You can use perception, self-awareness, and mood management strategies to make the right decisions, at the right place, at the right times, to excel in life. The first step is to learn how to manage your mood. Please provide solutions to the situations listed below.

When you are annoyed you will do this to improve your mood

_____

When you are angry you will do this to improve your mood

_____

When you are depressed you will do this to improve your mood

_____

When you are disrespected you are going to do this to improve your mood

_____

When you don't feel like exercising you're going to do this to put you in the mood

_____

When you don't feel like taking out the trash you're going to do this to put you in the mood

_____

When you feel like using alcohol or drugs you are going to do this to change your mood

_____

When you don't feel like controlling your mouth you're going to do this to change your mood

_____

When you are bored you are going to do this to keep your mind occupied

_____

When you don't feel like studying you're going to do this to change your mood

_____

When you don't feel like going to work you're going to do this to change your mood

_____

When you are sleepy and you need to wake up, you are going to do this

_____

When you are lonely you are going to make this healthy choice

_____

When you are low on money, you are going to do this

_____

When your heart is broken you're going to this

_____

When you're running late you're going to do this

_____

Add your own personal scenarios below that may occur in your life. After you write them, write down how you are going to deal with them in a healthy manner.

_____

COMPETITION

Many of us have heard statements like "I will drink you under the table" or have played games like beer pong. Competition is involved in many aspects of our life and can influence our choices. If we are not careful, competing in the wrong situations can develop negative habits or addictions.

1. How does competition at work influence substance use?

_____

_____

_____

_____

_____

_____

_____

2. Do you think that competition is good?

_____

_____

_____

_____

_____

_____

3. Is it okay to use drugs to enhance your abilities? Is it okay to use them to improve mood, focus, or performance in or outside of the workplace? Examples: Amphetamines, Cocaine, Beta Blockers, Steroids.

_____

_____

_____

_____

_____

_____

_____

_____

4. Would you be mad at a person for misrepresenting themselves to date you for the sake of competition? Ex. (Male enhancement pills, fake hair, fake nails, fake butt, fake muscles, fake persona, etc.)

_____

_____

_____

_____

_____

_____

_____

_____

_____

5. Can using drugs or alcohol become a competitive? If so, is it smart?

_____

_____

_____

_____

_____

_____

_____

_____

_____

6. Many people use drugs and alcohol because it is the only thing that is consistent or reliable. Many can depend on the mood altering effects from drugs or alcohol, more than they can depend on family, friends, and co-workers. What other ways can you achieve consistency in your life?

_____

_____

_____

_____

_____

_____

_____

7. Many chose to compete in areas of their life that will eventually harm them in the long run and tarnish their reputation (Excessive spending, partying, getting high, risky sexual behavior, lying, cheating, etc.) In what areas in your life should you compete?

_____

_____

_____

_____

_____

_____

_____

_____

_____

_____

_____

_____

_____

_____

BONDING

Many use drugs, alcohol, or cigarettes to start a conversation with other people. Some even ask this question, "Do you have a light?"

1. How has substance use become a part of your social life?

_____

_____

_____

_____

_____

_____

_____

2. Are there other ways to bond with people without using drugs or alcohol?

_____

_____

_____

_____

_____

_____

_____

3. Some people use substances to feel more comfortable in social situations. Many even have what we call "liquid courage." What can people do to increase their courage?

_____

_____

_____

_____

_____

_____

_____

_____

4. There are many who are addicted to the process of using. Lighting up, rolling a blunt, and placing something in one's mouth can be addicting. What alternatives can one use to reduce use of illegal substances?

_____

_____

_____

_____

_____

_____

_____

_____

_____

_____

_____

_____

_____

_____

_____

_____

_____

_____

_____

_____

_____

HABITS

Our thoughts become or beliefs, our beliefs become our actions, our actions become our habits, and our habits become our destiny.

List your good and bad habits below

Good	Bad

What will your potential destiny be if you continue to keep your bad habits?

_____

_____

_____

_____

_____

_____

What good habits would you like to add?

_____

_____

_____

_____

_____

_____

List the benefits of eliminating your bad habits

_____

_____

_____

_____

_____

_____

_____

_____

_____

_____

_____

_____

_____

_____

_____

_____

_____

_____

_____

_____

_____

_____

_____

FAMILY DRAMA

1. How has your family affected your emotions?

_____

_____

_____

_____

_____

_____

_____

2. How has your family influenced your relationships with others?

_____

_____

_____

_____

_____

_____

_____

3. Which family member can "push your buttons" the most? What do they do?

_____

_____

_____

_____

_____

_____

_____

_____

4. What strategies do other people use in your family to deal with the person mentioned on the previous page?

_____

_____

_____

_____

_____

_____

_____

5. Do they push your buttons because you keep responding to it? How can you change the effect that it has on you?

_____

_____

_____

_____

_____

_____

_____

6. How has family secrets affected your life positively or negatively?

_____

_____

_____

_____

_____

_____

_____

_____

7. Is denial about substance, sexual, verbal, or physical abuse acceptable within the family? Should this history of behavior be hidden from family members? Why or why not?

_____

_____

_____

_____

_____

_____

_____

8. Should accomplishments, awards, promotions, or scholarships be hidden from family members? Why or why not?

_____

_____

_____

_____

_____

_____

_____

9. How can you improve your family?

_____

_____

_____

_____

_____

_____

_____

_____

10. Is family something that you value? If so, in what ways do you show that you value your family? Are you improving your family or are you keeping the family drama alive?

_____

_____

_____

_____

_____

_____

_____

11. Would you raise your children the same way your parents raised you? If not, what changes would you make?

_____

_____

_____

_____

_____

_____

_____

_____

_____

_____

_____

_____

LET IT GO

1. What is the purpose of holding on to the past?

_____

_____

_____

_____

_____

_____

_____

2. Where does "holding on to the past" get you?

_____

_____

_____

_____

_____

_____

_____

3. Is your past affecting you presently? If so, how?

_____

_____

_____

_____

_____

_____

_____

_____

_____

4. Does holding on to negative things in your past benefit you in any way?

_____

_____

_____

_____

_____

_____

_____

_____

5. Seriously, does being negative or pessimistic lead to positive results?

_____

_____

_____

_____

_____

_____

_____

_____

6. If no, why do people continue to do it?

_____

_____

_____

_____

_____

_____

_____

_____

_____

7. What are the characteristics of victims?

_____

_____

_____

_____

_____

_____

_____

_____

_____

8. Do those characteristics describe you? Would you like to be held in eternal bondage by your past? Do you choose to be a victim for the rest of your life or will you choose to move forward and make the most of your future?

_____

_____

_____

_____

_____

_____

_____

INSTANT GRATIFICATION

Instant gratification can have a lasting impact on one's life. Listed below are some examples of instant gratification.

Drugs

Alcohol

Fast Food

Microwave

Gambling

Prostitution

Self-Checkout

Plastic Surgery

Payday Loans

Title Loans

Overnight Shipping

Shoplifting

Energy Drinks

Anticipation Loans (Taxes)

Autopay

Cell Phones

Crash Diets

Steroids

Wigs/ Weaves/ Extensions/Toupees

Girdles

Spray-on Tans

Please provide your own examples of instant gratification below.

_____

_____

_____

_____

_____

_____

_____

_____

_____

_____

_____

_____

DELAYED GRATIFICATION

1. How has instant gratification affected your life?

_____

_____

_____

_____

_____

_____

_____

2. What are the benefits of delayed gratification?

_____

_____

_____

_____

_____

_____

_____

3. What are the cons of instant gratification?

_____

_____

_____

_____

4. Are fast things good for you? Please explain.

5. Do good things come to those who wait? Please explain.

ANGER MANAGEMENT

1. How do you deal with anger? Do you fight, run away, or hold things in?

_____

_____

_____

_____

2. What is your best strategy to remove anger that does not involve substance use?

_____

_____

_____

_____

3. What strategies do you use when you are engaged in conflicts with different types of personalities?
   - ✓ Those who are aggressive
   - ✓ Those who are passive aggressive
   - ✓ Those who avoid conflict
   - ✓ Those who are silent
   - ✓ Those who hold grudges
   - ✓ Those who are in power positions

Aggressive_____

Passive Aggressive_____

Those who avoid conflict_____

Those who are silent_____

Those who hold grudges_____

Those who are in power positions_____

Anger Management Strategies

- ➢ Exercise
- ➢ Remove yourself from the event that is triggering you.
- ➢ Meditation
- ➢ Change your perception of the situation.
- ➢ Listen to music or watch something funny that changes your mood.
- ➢ Work on personal and professional goals.
- ➢ Try to see the "big picture" and be rational.
- ➢ Understand how prescription drugs affect your body.
- ➢ Don't engage in conversations with those you are not comfortable with. Example: (politics or religion)
- ➢ Know yourself and what you can handle. Place yourself in the best position for success.
- ➢ Get adequate food and rest.
- ➢ Be financially responsible.
- ➢ Let go of the past.
- ➢ Stop drug or alcohol use.
- ➢ Take alternate routes when dealing with traffic.
- ➢ Plan ahead of time
- ➢ Self-Care (Massages, Vacations, Grooming)
- ➢ Draw, color, or journal

PICK YOUR BATTLES

Write down an example of a time that you were emotional about a situation and it ended up making your life more difficult. Were you rational or irrational?

_____

_____

_____

_____

_____

_____

What did you learn from this situation?

_____

_____

_____

_____

_____

_____

_____

_____

_____

_____

_____

_____

_____

_____

_____

FEAR

FEAR stands for: false existence appearing real.

1. What are you afraid of?

_____

_____

_____

_____

2. What is your greatest fear? _____

3. What has fear stopped you from doing?

_____

_____

_____

_____

4. How has fear impacted your life?

_____

_____

_____

_____

5. Imagine the best possible outcome after you face your fear? What is the best that can happen?

_____

_____

_____

_____

FINANCIAL CONSEQUENCES

Fines $_____

Income lost from not working $_____

Legal Fees (Probation/Court/Lawyer) $_____

Drug and Alcohol Evaluation $_____

Alcohol and Drug Classes/ASAM Treatment $_____

Childcare $_____

Gas $_____

Food bought while taking classes $_____

Loss of wages $_____

Repair bills or restitution $_____

TOTAL MONEY LOST $_____

Hours in court   _____

Hours in probation   _____

Hours doing community service   _____

Hours in jail   _____

Hours in class   _____

Other hours lost   _____

TOTAL TIME LOST   _____

TIME x HOURLY WAGE = VALUE OF TIME LOST

_____ X $_____ = $_____

VALUE OF TIME LOST $_____

VALUE OF TIME LOST + TOTAL MONEY LOSS= $_____

WAS IT WORTH IT? _____

TRUTHFULNESS

1. Can women handle the truth? Why or why not?

   _____

   _____

   _____

   _____

2. Can men handle the truth? Why or why not?

   _____

   _____

   _____

   _____

3. What are things that women lie about?

   _____

   _____

   _____

   _____

4. What are things that men lie about?

   _____

   _____

   _____

   _____

5. Who are better liars? Women or men?

   _____

   _____

6. How do women lie differently than men? How do they cover it up? What tactics do they use?

_____

_____

_____

_____

7. What do addicts lie about? What tactics do they use?

_____

_____

_____

_____

8. Do you respect liars? Why or why not?

_____

_____

_____

_____

9. Do you lie to yourself? If so, why?

_____

_____

_____

_____

10. What is a purpose of a lie?

_____

_____

_____

_____

11. past?

_____

_____

_____

_____

12.   Strip away your ego, defenses, and lies you tell yourself. Truly, who are you?

_____

_____

_____

_____

DECISION TREE

In life, we are required to make a lot of decisions, both big and small. Each choice we make will have a ripple effect on many different aspects of our life that we may have failed to consider. This is why it is very important to evaluate our choices in order to create the best possible outcomes.

Creating a decision tree helps you see the possible ripple effects of your choices.

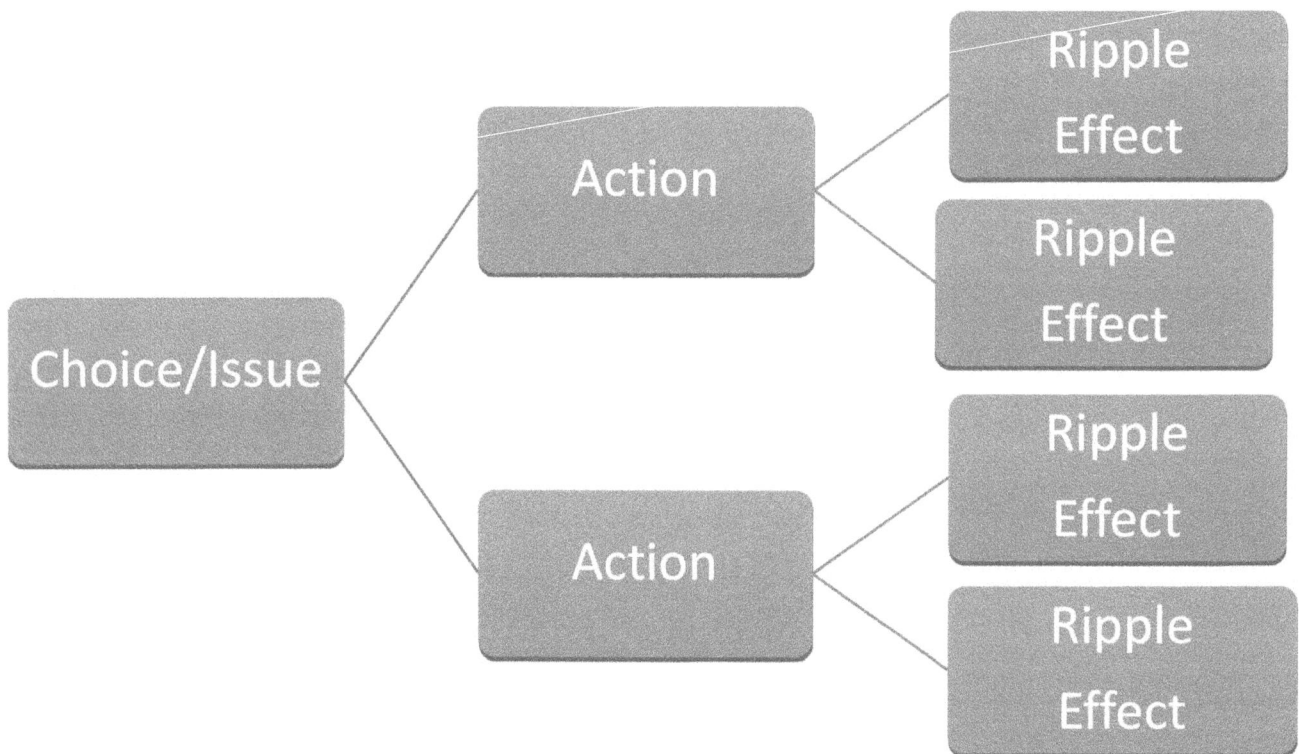

```
                                              ┌─────────┐
                                              │ Ripple  │
                                              │ Effect  │
                              ┌──────────┐    └─────────┘
                              │  Action  │
                              └──────────┘    ┌─────────┐
                                              │ Ripple  │
                                              │ Effect  │
        ┌──────────────┐
        │ Choice/Issue │
        └──────────────┘
                                              ┌─────────┐
                                              │ Ripple  │
                              ┌──────────┐    │ Effect  │
                              │  Action  │    └─────────┘
                              └──────────┘
                                              ┌─────────┐
                                              │ Ripple  │
                                              │ Effect  │
                                              └─────────┘
```

Sample Decision Tree

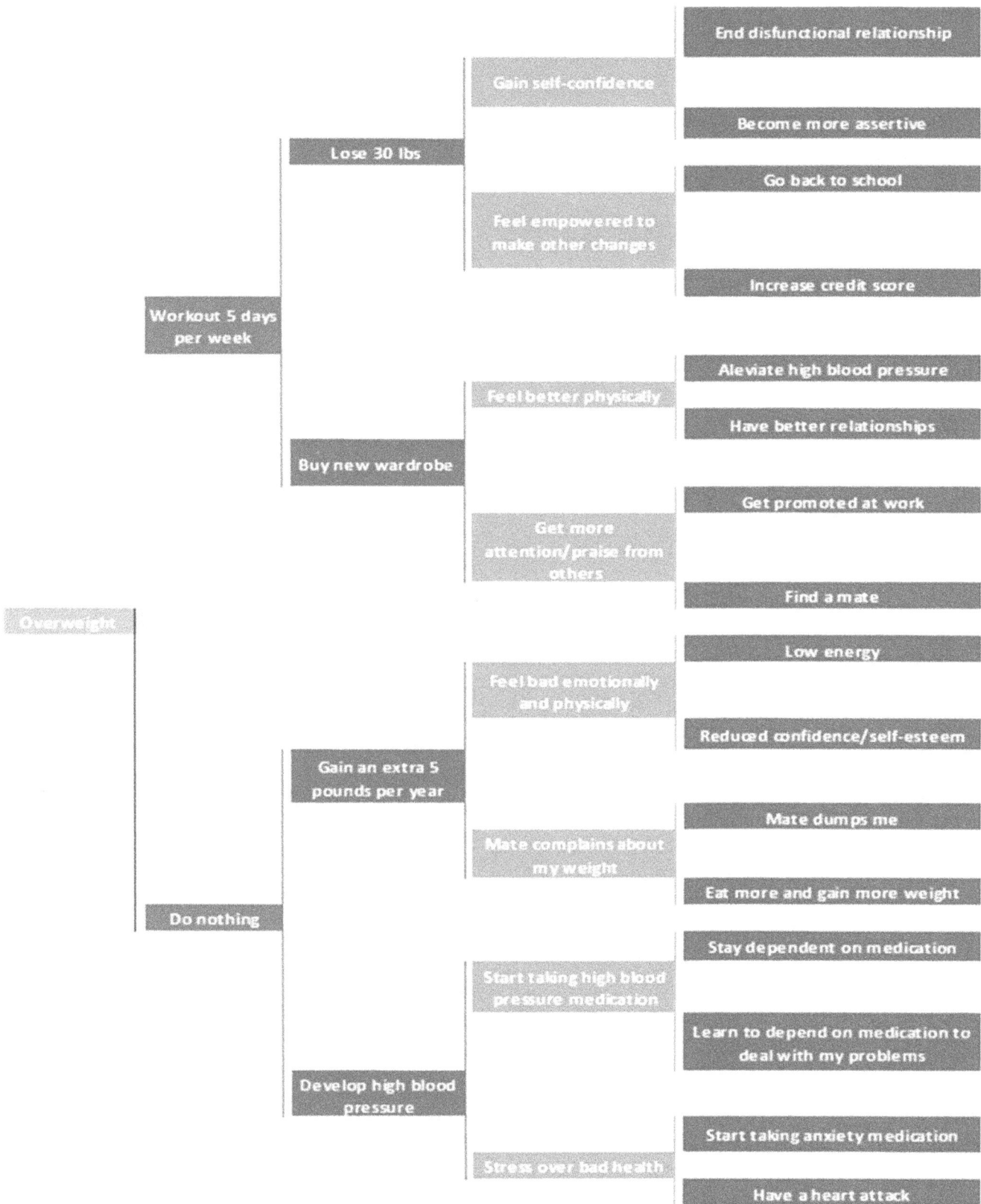

Please create your own decision tree and evaluate your choices on this page.

SELF-AWARENESS

1. What makes you feel happy, relaxed, and fulfilled?

_____

_____

_____

_____

_____

_____

2. What are the top three distractions or weaknesses that keep you from achieving your goals? How will you remove these weaknesses or distractions?

_____

_____

_____

_____

_____

_____

3. What are your strengths? Are there other skills that you need to develop? If so, what are they?

_____

_____

_____

_____

_____

_____

4. Pretend that you were told by your doctor that you had five years to live. How would you change your life? Would you do anything differently?

_____

_____

_____

_____

_____

_____

5. What do you want to be known for? What kind of legacy will you leave behind?

_____

_____

_____

_____

_____

_____

6. Describe the characteristics of your ideal mate. What kind of personality does he/she have? What are his/her physical characteristics? What are deal breakers for you?

Personality	Physical Features	Deal Breakers	Other

7. What was the best birthday you ever had? What did you do and who was there?

_____

_____

_____

_____

_____

_____

8. Who do you admire and respect? What qualities do they have and what do you need to do to get those same qualities?

_____

_____

_____

_____

_____

1. Name: _____ Relationship: _____

Qualities: _____

2. Name: _____ _____Relationship: _____

Qualities: _____

9. If you could be any fictional character, who would you be and why?

_____

_____

_____

_____

10. If you had a million dollars right now, how would you spend or invest it? Be specific.

_____

_____

_____

_____

_____

CREDIT

So what is credit anyway? In essence, credit is any form of delayed payment. It allows one party (the debtor or borrower) to receive money, goods, or services from another party (the creditor or lender) without having to pay up front.

Instead there is an agreement based on trust that the borrower will either pay or return the materials (or other materials of equal value) at a later date. The cost of credit comes in the form of a predetermined rate of interest that is applied to the amount borrowed and will accrue until the debt has been paid.

Common forms of credit include:

- Mortgages
- Personal loans
- Credit Cards
- Store Cards
- Automobile loans

Credit bureaus collect information from various sources regarding your borrowing and bill-paying habits and create a report based on these findings. A credit score is a number that represents your credit worthiness. It is formulated based on your credit report. The most common credit scores are FICO scores. FICO scores range from 300 – 850. The higher the score, the better your credit. Your credit score is used to determine whether you are worthy of credit, to determine interest rates, and assess your ability to pay back loans. In essence, your past behavior is used to predict your future behavior. Because credit is based on trust and your previous financial behavior, it is very important to create a flawless track record of bill paying activity.

1. Do you know your credit score? If so, what is it?

_____

_____

_____

_____

_____

_____

2. When was the last time you checked your credit score and credit report?

_____

_____

_____

_____

_____

_____

3. Do you typically pay your bills on time? Why or why not?

_____

_____

_____

_____

_____

4. How many lines of credit do you have open (credit cards, loans, etc.)?

_____

_____

_____

_____

_____

5. Are your credit cards maxed out? If so, why?

_____

_____

_____

_____

_____

6. Do you pay the minimum amount allowed? If so, why?

_____

_____

_____

_____

_____

_____

7. How soon do you think you will be able to pay off your credit cards?

_____

_____

_____

_____

_____

The United States has 3 national credit bureaus:

- Equifax
- Experian
- TransUnion

8. Do you have a plan in place to pay off your debts? If so, what is it?

_____

_____

_____

_____

_____

9. How can you improve your credit? (FYI, having no credit is bad credit)

_____

_____

_____

_____

_____

PERSONAL BUDGET

Many people become angry, depressed, or stressed out due to poor financial management. On this page, create a monthly budget for yourself based on your current income.

Mortgage/Rent:

_____

Utilities:

_____

Groceries:

_____

Insurance:

_____

Cell Phone:

_____

Internet:

_____

Credit Card:

_____

Entertainment/Self Care:

_____

Clothing:

_____

Gas:

_____

Misc.:

_____

Savings:

_____

Money in	- Money out	= Money left

Notes:

_____

_____

_____

_____

At the height of your substance use how much money were you spending on alcohol or drugs in a week?

_____

At the height of your substance use how much money were you spending on alcohol and drugs in a month?

_____

At the height of your substance use how much money were you spending on alcohol and drugs in a year?

_____

What could you have accomplished with this money instead of using it for alcohol or drugs?

_____

DECISION MAKING SCENARIOS

Each decision or choice that you make has a ripple effect. We would like for you to practice your decision making skills while being exposed to emotionally charged scenarios. There are no right or wrong answers. We just want you to practice making decisions while being emotionally charged.

If you want to get better at singing, public speaking, driving a car, painting, or doing some other skill, you need to practice. People who live the best lives make the best decisions. We want you to make the best decisions for your life.

On the next page, there is a series of scenarios for you to evaluate. Please have a response for each scenario listed. Please keep it real and don't give answers that you think your group or counselor want to hear. Remember this is a judgment free zone.

Scenario # 1

While on a 15-minute break during group, a fellow client tells you that their last day is next week but they are afraid that they will fail the final drug test that is required to complete treatment. They ask if they can use your urine because you have been completely abstinent. What would you do?

_____

_____

_____

_____

Scenario # 2

You are a mother/father of three children. You're offered a spot on a popular reality show. The pay is $20,000 per episode. The show is very popular and known for having a lot of fights, arguments, and undignified behavior. In order to be on the show you must behave the same way (i.e., argue and fight, tell the world all your deep dark secrets, sexualize yourself, let people disrespect you, disrespect others and show the worst sides of yourself). What would you do?

_____

_____

_____

_____

Scenario # 3

You're watching the news and you see video footage of a man that is wanted by the police for murdering a woman and burning her body on the side of the road near your house. The man looks exactly like your brother. Just a week before, on the night of the murder, your brother came to your house looking worried and asking for a gas can. Although you didn't give him your gas can, you noticed later on that it was missing. What would you do?

_____

_____

_____

_____

Scenario # 4

You are at a family gathering and your cousin has brought his new girlfriend. You notice that he is being verbally abusive to her (i.e., calling her out of her name, saying disrespectful things and threatening to beat her up). What do you do?

_____

_____

_____

_____

Scenario # 5

While on vacation in a foreign country, someone offers you a "Molly" (MDMA) while you are partying in the club. How do you handle this situation?

_____

_____

_____

_____

Scenario # 6

You are on probation and your supervisor needs a ride home. He uses cocaine on a regular basis and is known to have cocaine on him at all times. Do you give him a ride home?

_____

_____

_____

_____

_____

Scenario # 7

School is about to start and you just bought some new school clothes for your daughter. While she waits at the bus stop, a neighborhood bully rips her clothes and harasses her. Your daughter reports this back to you and you find out that this bully's parent is your supervisor at your job. How do you handle this situation?

_____

_____

_____

_____

_____

Scenario # 8

You are struggling financially and your neighbor is "getting over" because she is getting disability, food stamps, and a tax return for three kids that are not hers. Plus she has a babysitting business next door and is not licensed by the state to run a daycare.

1. Do you report her?
2. Do you blackmail her to get a cut of her money?
3. Do you ignore the situation and mind your business?
4. Other_____

Scenario # 9

Your mom is single and she is dating someone who is the same age as you. They invite you to dinner where he proposes to her and she gladly accepts. They have been only dating for a month. Later that evening, he comes to you and asks for your blessing and support of his marriage to your mom. How do you handle this situation?

_____

_____

_____

_____

_____

Scenario # 10

You get laid off from work and receive your final check. With this check you now have a total of $800 left to your name to pay your $700 rent, $300 car note, and $200 in utility bills. It is your daughter's sixth birthday next week. How do you handle this situation? What will be your strategy?

_____

_____

_____

_____

_____

Scenario # 11

You are hanging out at your friend's house watching football and he decides to invite more people over to watch the game. These are all of the people that you used to drink and drug with before you entered treatment. How will you handle this situation?

_____

_____

_____

_____

_____

Scenario # 12

You just came home from a long day that included a visit with your probation officer. You are stressed out about the things going on in your life at the moment and you would like nothing more than to use drugs/alcohol to help you relax. You know you have 30 days until your next appointment with your probation officer so the alcohol/drug may be out of your system by then. What do you do?

_____

_____

_____

_____

_____

Scenario # 13

You have just served 30 days in jail after receiving a probation violation for testing positive for alcohol/drugs. You had been completely abstinent until that point and only used because your long-term significant other influenced you to use with him/her. You do not want any more legal problems so you ask your significant other to support you by abstaining from alcohol/drugs while in your presence, but he/she refuses. What do you do?

_____

_____

_____

_____

_____

Scenario # 14

You and your co-worker were given a joint project to complete but your co-worker was lazy and you ended up doing all the work. When it was time to present to your boss your co-worker took over the presentation and made it seem like they were the leader on it. Your boss then praised your co-worker and said nothing to you. How do you handle this situation?

_____

_____

_____

_____

_____

Scenario #15

A known drug dealer offers you $50,000 to transport some drugs from Atlanta to New York. You just graduated from college and this amount of money will pay off your student loans. What do you do?

_____

_____

_____

_____

_____

CRIMINAL THINKING

There are those in recovery that attempt to "get over" or hustle the system due to criminal thinking. These thinking patterns have been developed over time and may have been introduced by friend, associate, co-worker, or family member. This type of thinking can be considered manipulative, sneaky, hostile, irrational, and morally or ethically wrong.

1. Do you have a criminal mind?

Yes or No

_____

_____

_____

_____

_____

_____

2. How does having a criminal mind add or decrease value to one's life?

_____

_____

_____

_____

_____

_____

3. Do you associate yourself with criminals? If so, why?

_____

_____

_____

_____

_____

_____

4. Are you willing to do time for something that someone else did?

_____

_____

_____

_____

_____

_____

_____

_____

5. Do you believe in snitching?

Yes or No

6. Is having a criminal reputation negative or positive?

_____

_____

_____

_____

_____

_____

_____

7. Why is snitching considered to be negative amongst criminals? I thought having a "rap sheet" improves criminal reputation?

_____

_____

_____

_____

_____

_____

8. Is living a criminal lifestyle stress free? What are the potential consequences of living this way?

_____

_____

_____

_____

_____

_____

_____

9. What are the principles that criminals live by? Do these principles protect your values?

_____

_____

_____

_____

_____

_____

_____

10. Many criminals say they don't have any other options and that is why they commit crimes. How is this true when there are examples of people who come from the same circumstances overcoming the same obstacles? Do criminals choose to be victims and make excuses? Or are they as strong as they claim to be?

_____

_____

_____

_____

_____

_____

_____

MINDSET MAINTENANCE

✓ Know your triggers and stay away from them.

✓ Find alternate ways to cope.

✓ Go to counseling for un-resolved issues like grief, depression, anger, anxiety, substance use, or a gambling or sex addiction.

✓ Engage in activities that improve your mood (manage your emotions).

✓ Do positive things that you used to enjoy that you don't do now (nostalgia, music, hobbies, old television shows).

✓ Try something new and gain exposure to exciting things that interest you.

✓ Resolve personal issues with family, friends and coworkers.

✓ Be assertive and do not be afraid to tell people "no."

✓ Be aware and adjust your behavior patterns.

✓ Stay away from negative influences.

✓ Develop an action plan to improve emotionally, physically, and financially.

✓ Understand the long-term consequences of your actions and how it will affect you personally, professionally, and emotionally.

✓ Practice delayed gratification.

✓ Create a budget for yourself and only buy what you need and save for the future.

✓ When you have the urge to engage in negative behaviors, know that you have a choice. You are not on auto-pilot and you can control your behavior.

✓ Go to school and improve your marketability by earning a degree, trade, or license in a specialized field. Work on professional goals.

✓ Exercise regularly and try to get sunlight as much as possible to increase endorphins.

✓ Do positive things and engage in legal experiences that make you happy.

✓ Develop a relapse prevention plan. Pre-plan on how you are going to respond to stress, anxiety, failure, and mistakes in a positive manner that lead to long-term success.

TIME MANAGEMENT

Goals   Priority   Deadline

1. _____   _____   _____

2. _____   _____   _____

3. _____   _____   _____

4. _____   _____   _____

5. _____   _____   _____

Time   Activity   Time   Activity

_____   _____   _____   _____

Monday

_____   _____   _____   _____

_____   _____   _____   _____

_____   _____   _____   _____

_____   _____   _____   _____

Time   Activity   Time   Activity

_____   _____   _____   _____

Tuesday

_____   _____   _____   _____

_____   _____   _____   _____

_____   _____   _____   _____

_____   _____   _____   _____

Time   Activity   Time   Activity

_____   _____   _____   _____

Wednesday

_____   _____   _____   _____

_____   _____   _____   _____

_____   _____   _____   _____

_____   _____   _____   _____

Time   Activity   Time   Activity

_____   _____   _____   _____

Thursday

_____   _____   _____   _____

_____   _____   _____   _____

_____   _____   _____   _____

_____   _____   _____   _____

Time   Activity   Time   Activity

_____   _____   _____   _____

Friday

_____   _____   _____   _____

_____   _____   _____   _____

_____   _____   _____   _____

_____   _____   _____   _____

Time   Activity   Time   Activity

_____   _____   _____   _____

Saturday

_____   _____   _____   _____

_____   _____   _____   _____

_____   _____   _____   _____

_____   _____   _____   _____

Time	Activity		Time	Activity
_____	_____		_____	_____

Sunday

_____	_____		_____	_____
_____	_____		_____	_____
_____	_____		_____	_____
_____	_____		_____	_____

Time	Activity		Time	Activity
_____	_____		_____	_____

SETTING GOALS

Write a list of short-term and long-term goals that you would like to accomplish.

_____

_____

_____

_____

_____

_____

Transform your list of goals into SMART goals by answering the following questions. Start with the first goal listed above.

Goal:

_____

_____

_____

Specific: What specifically do you want to do?

_____

_____

_____

_____

_____

Measurable: How will you measure your success? How much? How many?

_____

_____

_____

Attainable: Is it in your power to accomplish this goal?

_____

_____

_____

Relevant: Is this goal consistent with your other goals and plans.

_____

_____

_____

Time-bound: What is the established deadline that will create a reasonable sense of urgency for you to complete the goal?

_____

_____

_____

SMART Goal:

_____

_____

_____

_____

_____

_____

PROFESSIONAL DEVELOPMENT

What can you specialize in that makes you different from the crowd? What special skill, niche, or talent can you develop that will put you in demand?

Homework Assignment:

Go on the internet and search for careers that require a special skill or training that you would be willing to commit to. Look for something that most people are not doing or thinking about. Look for apprenticeship and certification programs. Do not be discouraged if it requires you to jump through a lot of hoops. This element is created to weed out competition and the people who are not serious.

Sample Careers:

Food Stylist	Deep Sea Welding	Linguistics Specialist
Trauma Cleanup	Polygraph Examiner	Millwright
Toy Cleanup	Cremator	Water Damage Restoration
Demolition	Adult Daycare	Foley Artist

List the careers that you are interested in

_____

_____

_____

_____

_____

_____

SELF-CARE

There are those in this world who fail to take care of themselves. Due to this, they suffer at work, have poor relationships, live shorter lives, use illegal drugs to cope, etc. It is important that we take care of ourselves. Check the things that you would like to do to improve your self-care.

_____Massages

_____Vacation

_____Manicures

_____Pedicures

_____Facial

_____Staycation

_____Alone time

_____Sunlight

_____Exercise

_____Be in Nature

_____Socialize

_____Sex

_____Improve Living Environment

_____Improve Work Environment

_____Buy New Clothes

_____Sleep

_____Read

_____Improve Eating Habits

_____Hobbies

_____Get Counseling

Believe in Yourself

You need to believe that you can be sober and accomplish anything that you are trying to achieve.

Believability Scale

1_____2_____3_____4_____5_____6_____7_____8_____9_____10

On a scale of one to ten, one being the lowest and ten being the highest, circle the number that represents your belief that you will not be in this situation again. If you circle ten, that means you are very confident you will not be in this situation again. If you circle one, that means that you believe you will be in this situation again.

1. Explain why you chose the number you circled.

_____

_____

_____

_____

_____

_____

2. What can you do to increase your belief?

_____

_____

_____

_____

_____

_____

APPRECIATION

We sometimes forget about our blessings and take them for granted. It is important to appreciate the things that we have. When you think about complaining always remember that things can be worse. Believe it or not, there are people in this world that wish they were in your position.

List the things that you are thankful for.

_____   _____

_____   _____

_____   _____

_____   _____

People take care of the things that they truly appreciate. For example, if someone appreciates their car, they keep their car clean and make sure that they keep up on the maintenance. Appreciation is more than saying words. It is consists of feeling thankful and doing things that show that you are appreciative. Good things come when you appreciate what you already have.

List the things that you can do to show your appreciation.

_____

_____

_____

_____

_____

_____

SOBRIETY LOG

Place a checkmark for each day that you abstain from using alcohol or drugs. "Keep it real." Be honest when filling this out.

	Mon	Tues	Weds	Thurs	Fri	Sat	Sun
Week 1							
Week 2							
Week 3							
Week 4							
Week 5							
Week 6							
Week 7							
Week 8							
Week 9							
Week 10							
Week 11							
Week 12							
Week 13							
Week 14							
Week 15							
Week 16							
Week 17							
Week 18							
Week 19							
Week 20							
Week 21							
Week 22							

Week 23						
Week 24						
Week 25						
Week 26						
Week 27						
Week 28						
Week 29						
Week 30						
Week 31						
Week 32						
Week 33						
Week 34						
Week 35						
Week 36						
Week 37						
Week 38						
Week 39						
Week 40						
Week 41						
Week 42						
Week 43						
Week 44						
Week 45						
Week 46						
Week 47						
Week 48						
Week 49						
Week 50						
Week 51						
Week 52						

www.ingramcontent.com/pod-product-compliance
Lightning Source LLC
Chambersburg PA
CBHW042339030426

42335CB00030B/3406